# Casper and Daisy's
# Big Day at the Park

illustrated by Julia Seal

Look at these furry friends snoozing away,
**"But who are these doggies?"**
I hear you say.

The big boy is Casper.
He's so **strong** and **smart**,

The little lady is Daisy
with such a **big heart**!

This is no ordinary doggie duo. Casper dreams of becoming a **hero**.

He's not like other dogs that gnaw bones and chase sheep.

He has only one wish— he just wants to **speak**!

Instead of every day going for **walks**, they could sit down together for **talks**!

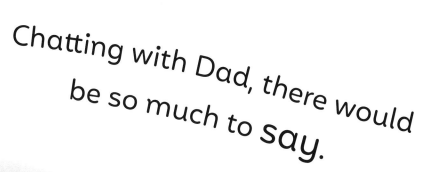

Chatting with Dad, there would be so much to **say**.

They'd share thoughts and ideas in between **play**.

As Casper lay dreaming, he woke with a start.
Daisy was heading off to the park.

The pair of pooches ran off at **high speed.**
Casper's long legs put him just in the lead.

In the park they ran all over the place until Casper landed flat on his **face**!

Some other dogs made fun of his fall.
They really weren't being nice at all.

When Dougal the cat wandered through,
the dogs picked on him for no reason, too.

While it's true their **bark**
was worse than their **bite**,

Dougal was still given a nasty fright.

The poor little kitty ran away feeling sad.
How could these doggies treat him so bad?

As Daisy helped Casper, they kept on being mean.
They were the worst doggies she had ever seen...

Suddenly something caught Daisy's eye.
It was **big** and **round**, and it fell from the sky.
A **bouncy** ball landed right there on the ground.
It was **pretty** and **patterned**,
and made barely a sound.

Rainbow letters from **A to Z** decorated the ball!
Daisy knew then and there it was the **best ball** of all.

As doggies must do, he gave the ball a good **chew**.
Then he flicked it to Daisy and she had a munch, too.

What happened next made the doggies **rejoice**.
Casper opened his mouth and out came a **voice**!

Daisy! I'm talking!
It's my dream come true!

We're speaking, Casper,
just like people do!

They couldn't believe what had just happened here,
until Casper told Daisy, "I have an idea!"

F V S M Y H D
O P W E X J N
T R I Q U L

"When we chewed the ball, our speaking was set.
I think we've just swallowed the **alphabet**!"

"You're right," Daisy agreed, turning back to the ball.
The bad doggies ran over—they had heard it all.
Their tails were **wagging** and their eyes were **agog**.
They had never before seen a talking dog.

They wanted to try to see if they had a voice
But the ball decided to make its own choice.

It bounced up in the air and disappeared in the **blue**.
And there was nothing the bad doggies could do.
They watched and gave only a **woof** and a **whine**.
Casper told them, "That ball was clearly a sign!"

You laughed at me when I fell down.
Now you've got nothing to show but a frown.
You don't try to help. You just hang around.
So you don't have a voice and you won't make a sound.

Being mean can never be fun.
It hurts others and then the damage is done.
That magic ball decided you shouldn't speak,
in case unkindness was all you would wreak.

The doggies wandered off with nothing to say.
One thing's for sure, they learned a lesson that day.
From that moment on, they had a **change of heart**.
Kindness gave them a brand new start.

Casper and Daisy were feeling so glad.
They couldn't wait to get back and tell Dad
about the magic ball and the incredible **story**.
This was truly their moment of **glory**!

"Dad! Dad! Listen to us! We can **speak**!"
"**Wow**!" shouted Dad, "That's the best news this week!"

"You know what they say?
Every dog has its day.
This must be it—things are
going your way!"

Words have **power** and they all agreed,
"Do right in the world. That's what we all need!"

"Let's get you online, so everyone can **hear** and **see**.
Your message of kindness is the best way to be."
Their new voices were a gift to do good,
to show warmth, love, and care—
and they **definitely** would...

01:32